yukismart.com/b/694355

body

тіло
tilo

head

голова
holova

face

обличчя
oblychchia

grow up

дорослішати

doroslishaty

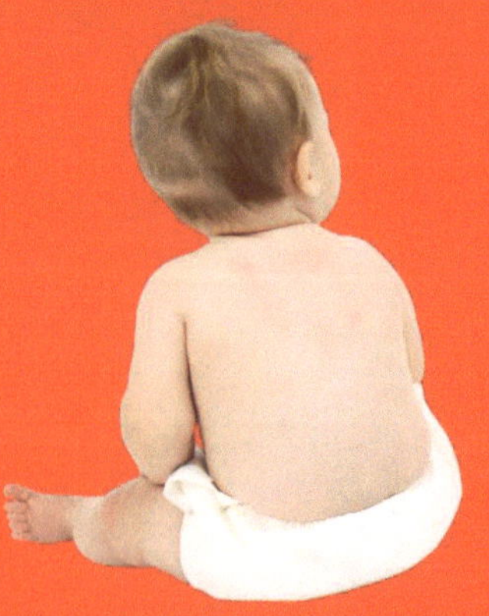

back

спина
spyna

chest

груди
hrudy

bottom

зад
zad

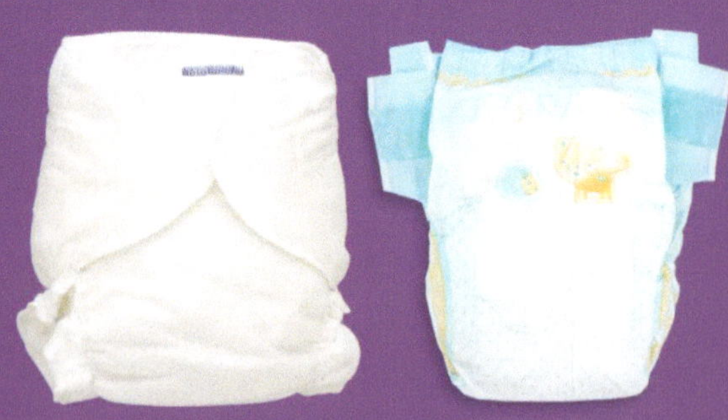

diaper

підгузник
pidhuznyk

eye

око
oko

glasses

окуляри
okuliary

forehead

лоб
lob

chin

підборіддя
pidboriddia

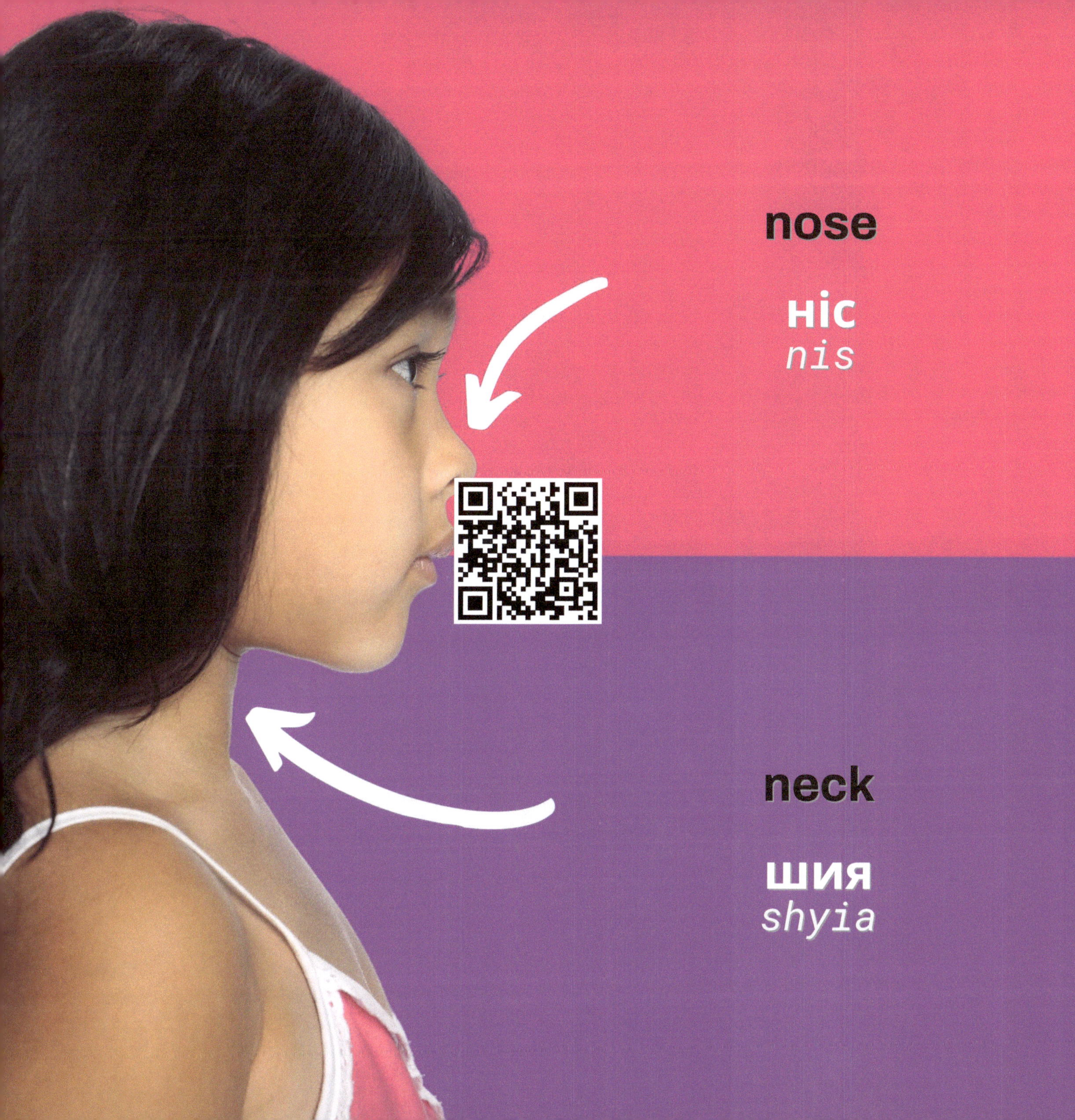

nose
ніс
nis
neck
шия
shyia

ear

вухо
vukho

cheeks

щоки
shchoky

kiss

поцілунок
potsilunok

mouth

рот
rot

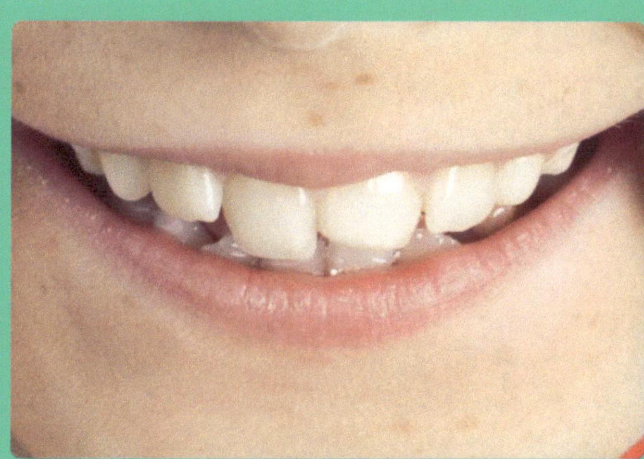

teeth

зуби
zuby

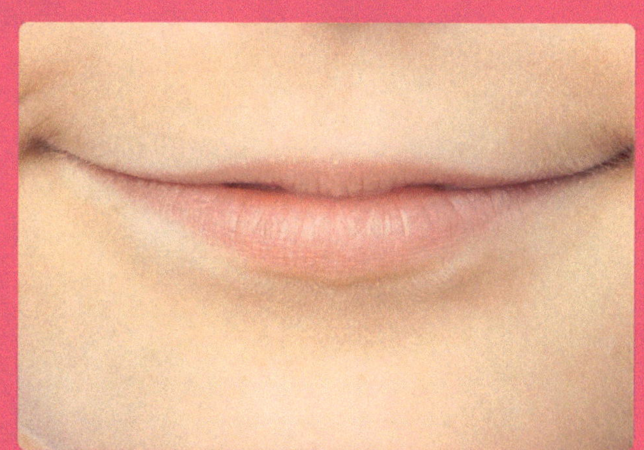

lips

губи
huby

tongue

ЯЗИК
iazyk

hair

ВОЛОССЯ
volossia

straight hair

пряме волосся

priame volossia

curly hair

кучеряве волосся

kucheriave volossia

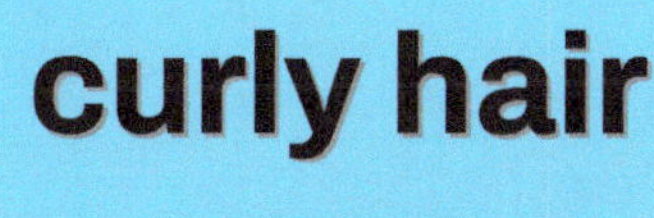

black hair

чорне волосся

chorne volossia

brown hair

каштанове волосся

kashtanove volossia

ginger hair

руде волосся

rude volossia

blond hair

світле волосся

svitle volossia

gray hair

сиве волосся

syve volossia

bald head

лиса голова

lysa holova

beard
борода
boroda
moustache
вуса
vusa

arm

передпліччя
peredplichchia

elbow

лікоть
likot

hand

кисть
kyst

fingers

пальці
paltsi

thumb

великий палець
velykyi palets

belly

живіт
zhyvit

navel

пупок
pupok

foot

стопа
stopa

leg

нога
noha

heel

п'ята
p'iata

thigh
стегно
stehno
ankle
щиколотка
shchykolotka

calf

литка
lytka

knee

коліно
kolino

nails

нігті
nihti

necklace

намисто
namysto

bracelet

браслет
braslet

hat

капелюх
kapeliukh

scarf

шарф
sharf

coat

пальто
palto

pullover

пуловер
pulover

pants

штани
shtany

dress

сукня
suknia

rain boots

гумові чоботи

humovi choboty

socks

шкарпетки

shkarpetky

shoes

черевики

cherevyky

mittens

рукавиці

rukavytsi

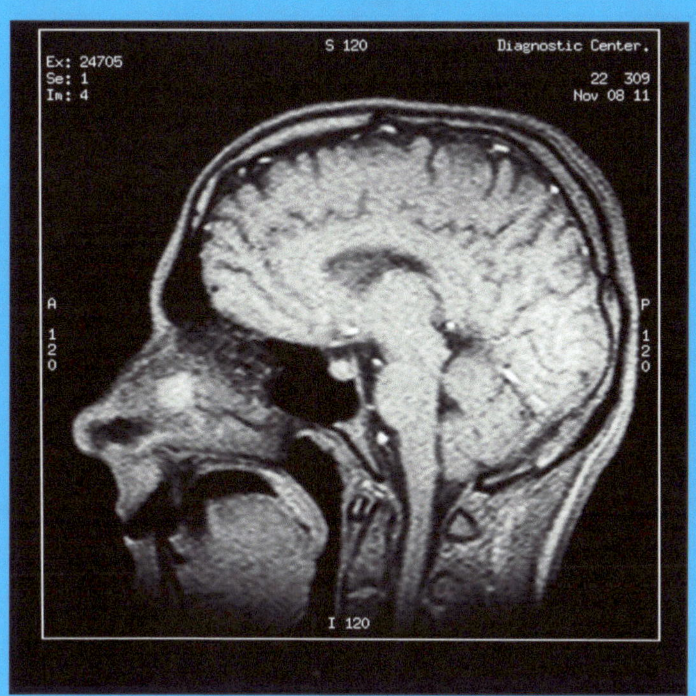

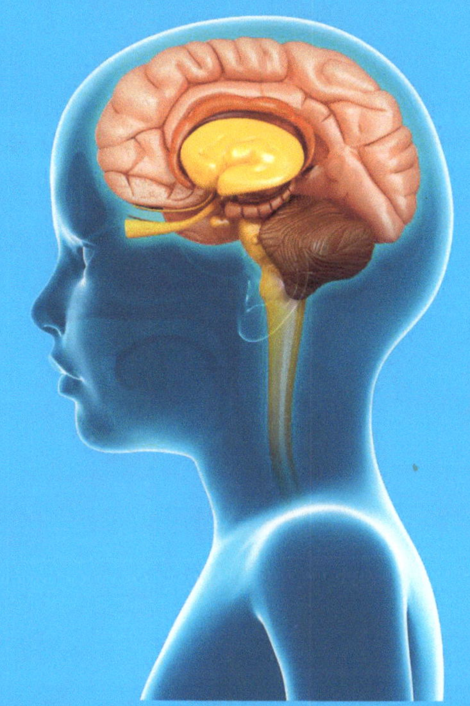

brain

МОЗОК
mozok

heart
серце
sertse
lungs
легені
leheni

skin

шкіра
shkira

sunscreen

сонцезахисний крем

sontsezakhysnyi krem

sun glasses

сонцезахисні окуляри

sontsezakhysni okuliary

soap

мило

mylo

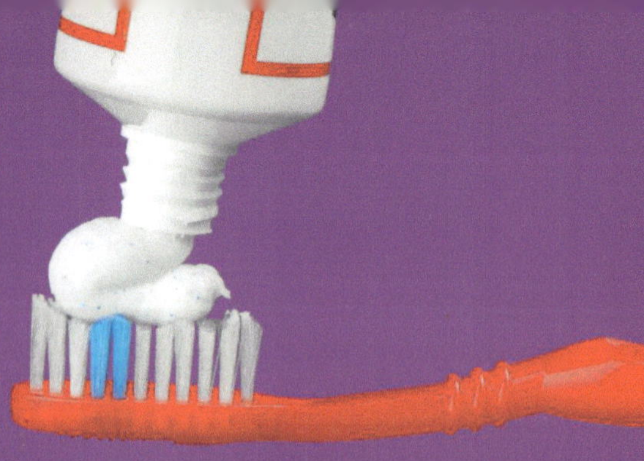

toothpaste

зубна паста

zubna pasta

toothbrush

зубна щітка

zubna shchitka

pain

біль
bil

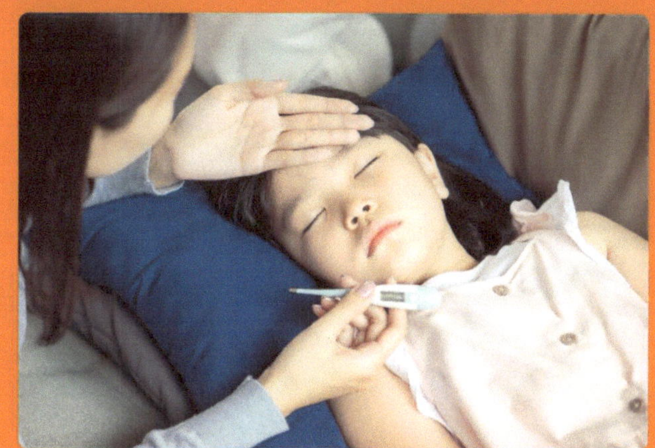

fever

гарячка
hariachka

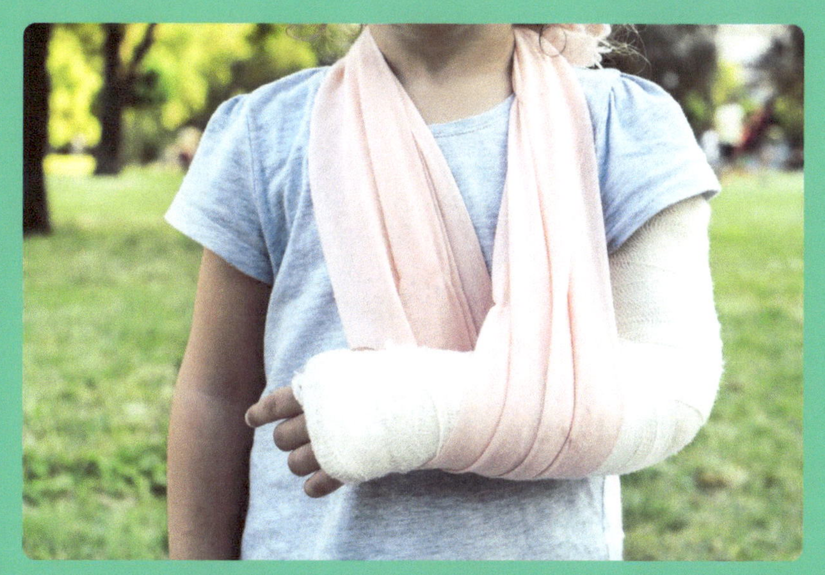

broken arm

зламана рука
zlamana ruka

sneeze

чхання
chkhannia

cough

кашель
kashel

dental cavity

карієс
kariies

pharmacist

фармацевт
farmatsevt

medicine

ліки
liky

hospital

лікарня
likarnia

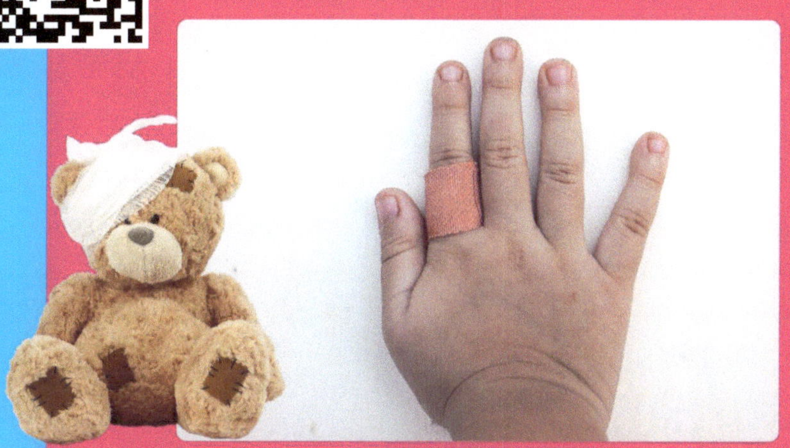

bandage

пластир
plastyr

paramedic

фельдшери
feldshery

firefighter

пожежник
pozhezhnyk

firetruck

пожежна машина

pozhezhna mashyna

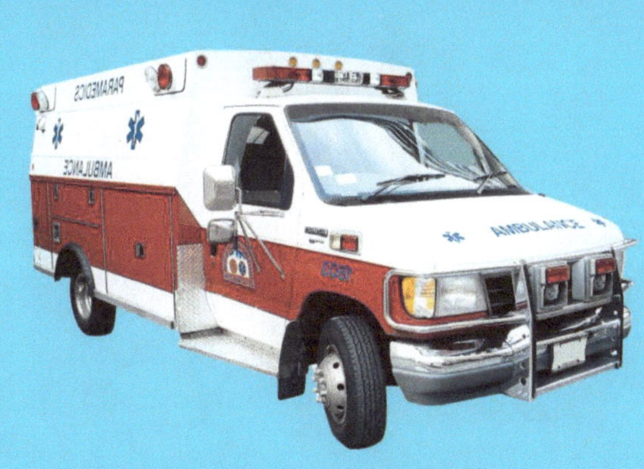

ambulance

швидка допомога

shvydka dopomoha

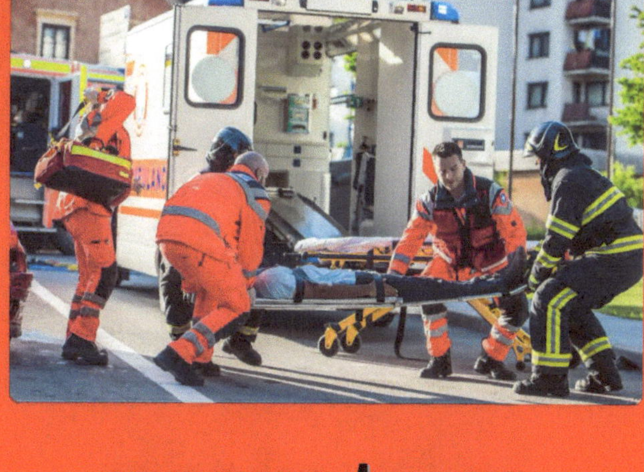

rescue team

команда рятувальників

komanda riatuvalnykiv

helicopter

вертоліт

vertolit

boat

човен

choven

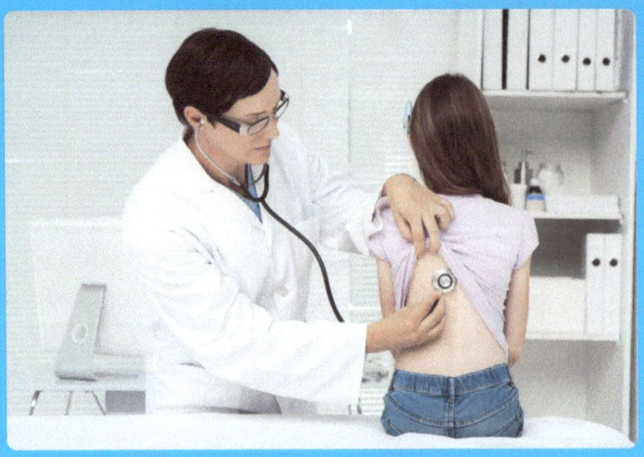

doctor

лікар
likar

nurse

медсестра
medsestra

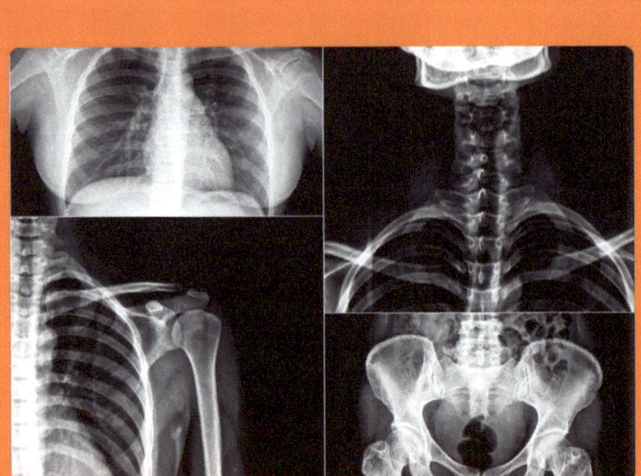

x-ray

рентген
renthen

wheelchair

інвалідний візок
invalidnyi vizok

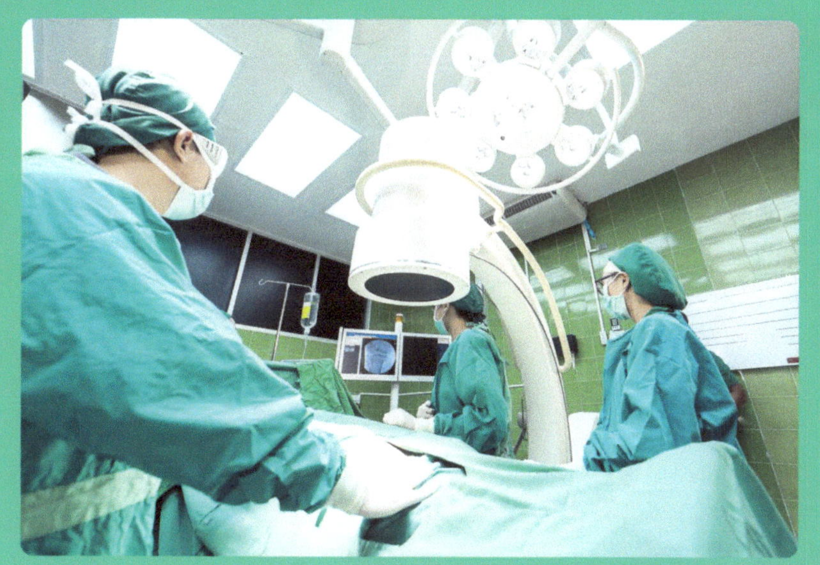

surgeon

хірург
khirurh

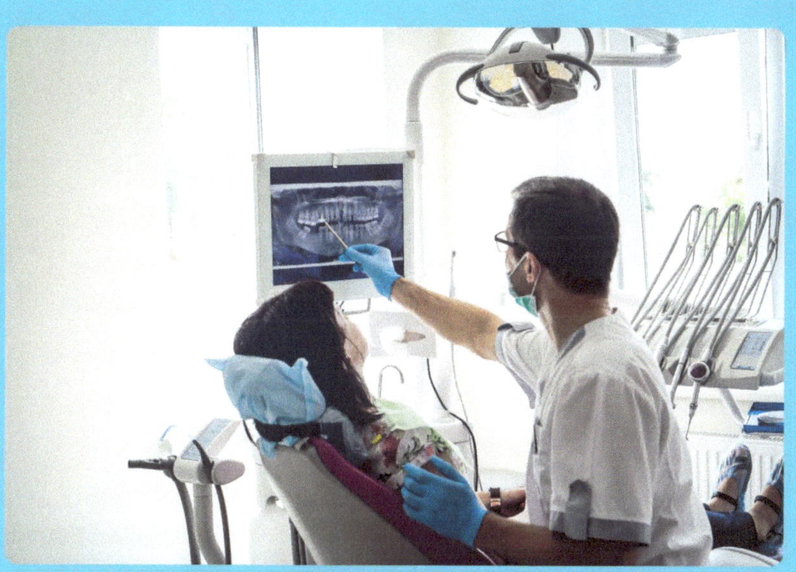

dentist

дантист
dantyst

thermometer

термометр
termometr

scale

ваги
vahy

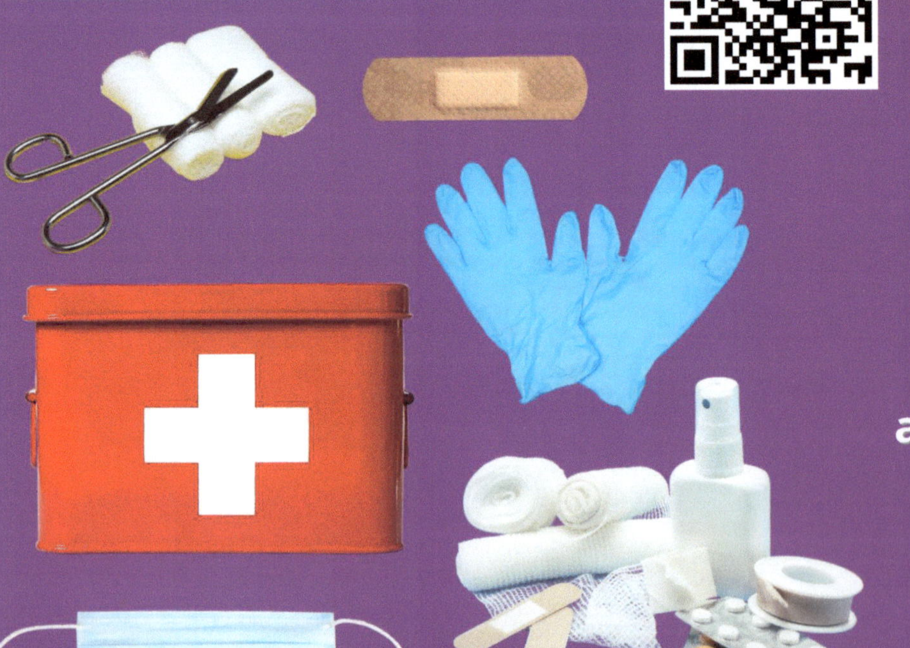

first aid kit

аптечка першої допомоги
aptechka pershoi dopomohy

vet

ветеринар
veterynar

stethoscope

стетоскоп
stetoskop

dancing

танці
tantsi

basketball

баскетбол
basketbol

soccer

футбол
futbol

swimming

плавання
plavannia

skiing

лижний спорт
lyzhnyi sport

judo

дзюдо
dziudo

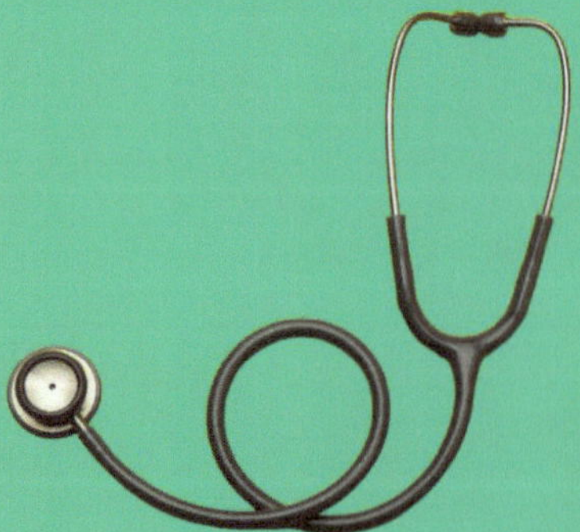

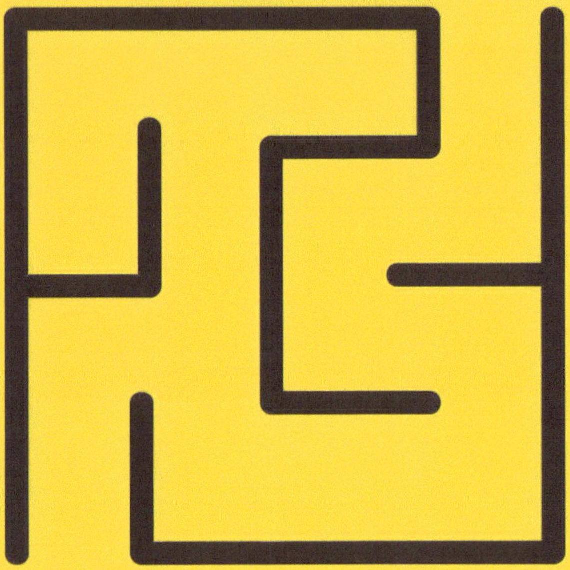